I0359899

Fashion by Design

Fashion by Design
Essentials for a Classic Wardrobe

Susan Bolding

PUBLISHING
& associates

Copyright

Unless otherwise indicated, all Scripture quotations are taken from the New King James Version of the Bible, copyright © 1979, 1980, 1982, Thomas Nelson, Inc., Publishers.

All Scripture quotations marked KJV are taken from the King James Version of the Bible.

Scriptures marked NLT are taken from the HOLY BIBLE, NEW LIVING TRANSLATION (NLT): Scriptures taken from the HOLY BIBLE, NEW LIVING TRANSLATION, Copyright© 1996, 2004, 2007 by Tyndale House Foundation. Used by permission of Tyndale House Publishers, Inc., Carol Stream, Illinois 60188. All rights reserved. Used by permission.

Scriptures marked AMP are taken from the AMPLIFIED BIBLE (AMP): Scripture taken from the AMPLIFIED® BIBLE, Copyright © 1954, 1958, 1962, 1964, 1965, 1987 by the Lockman Foundation Used by Permission. (www.Lockman.org)

Scriptures marked NIV are taken from the NEW INTERNATIONAL VERSION (NIV): Scripture taken from THE HOLY BIBLE, NEW INTERNATIONAL VERSION ®. Copyright© 1973, 1978, 1984, 2011 by Bi

Fashion by Design
Essentials for a Classic Wardrobe

ISBN: 978-1-944566-68-5

Copyright © 2024 by Susan Bolding

Bush Publishing & Associates, LLC books may be ordered at everywhere and at Amazon.com

For further information, please contact:
Bush Publishing & Associates
Tulsa, Oklahoma
www.bushpublishing.com

Printed in the United States of America.

No portion of this book may be used or reproduced by any means: graphic, electronic or mechanical, including photocopying, recording, taping, or by any information storage retrieval system, without the written permission of the publisher, except in the case of brief quotations embodied in critical articles and reviews.

Dedication

This book is dedicated to my husband Jimmy, the love of my life, my best friend, and my everyday encourager, who always helps me reach higher than I could have ever dreamed.

Fashion by Design

Notable Biblical women who had essentials for a classic wardrobe...

1.	Miriam	Praise & Worship Leader	Exodus 15:20
2.	Deborah	Patriotic Military Advisor	Judges 4:4-10
3.	Ruth	Woman of Constancy	Ruth 1:16
4.	Hannah	Ideal Mother	I Samuel 1:20
5.	Shunammite	Mrs. Hospitality	2 Kings 4:8
6.	Huldah	God's Confidant	2 Kings 22:14
7.	Queen Esther	Risk Taker	Esther 4:16

But the lady in Proverbs 31 excels them all! How? Every area and relationship of her life was permeated with her spiritual and practical devotion to God. Her excellent resume discloses her secret; her reverent and worshipful fear of the Lord.

Table of Contents

Dedication	vii
Fashion by Design	ix
Introduction	xiii

Chapter One — 1
Miriam Models a Garment of Praise — 3

Chapter Two — 7
Deborah, A Woman of Strength — 9

Chapter Three — 11
Ruth, Woman of Constancy — 13

Chapter Four — 17
Hannah the Ideal Mother — 19

Chapter Five — 25
The Shunammite, Mrs. Hospitality — 27

Chapter Six — 31
Huldah, Trusted with God's Secret — 33

Chapter Seven — 37
Esther, Risk Taker — 39

About the Author	43
Conclusion	44
Prayer	45

Introduction

    A few years ago, I noticed a footnote at the end of Proverbs 31:29 in the Amplified Bible. It read, "Many daughters have done... nobly and well... but you excel them all." What a glowing description of this woman in private life, this "capable, intelligent, and virtuous woman" of Proverbs 31! It means she had done more than Miriam, the one who led a nation's women in praise to God (Exodus 15:20, 21); more than Deborah, the patriotic military advisor (Judges 4:4-10); more than Ruth, the woman of constancy (Ruth 1:16); more than Hannah, the ideal mother (I Samuel 1:20; 2:19); more than the Shunammite, the hospitable woman (II Kings 4:8-10); more than Huldah, the woman who revealed God's secret message to national leaders (II Kings 22:14); and even more than Queen Esther, the woman who risked sacrificing her life for her people (Esther 4:16). Now, in what way exactly did she "excel them all"? In her spiritual and practical devotion to God, which permeated every area and relationship of her life. All seven of the Christian virtues (II Peter 1:5) are there, like colored threads in a tapestry. Her secret, which is open to everyone, is the Holy Spirit's climax to the story and to this book. In Proverbs 31:30, it becomes clear that the "reverent and worshipful fear of the Lord," which is "the beginning (the chief and choice part) of Wisdom" (Proverbs 9:10), is put forth as the true foundation for a life valued by God and her husband as "far above rubies or pearls" (Proverbs 31:10).

    Each of these women made a great contribution to our Bible heritage, and I was intrigued by the idea that it was the spiritual and practical devotion to God that gave them this place of distinction. As I began to study them, I began to see that each one could be compared to something in a lady's wardrobe—making this a unique way to learn about Christian virtues.

Our lives display the dealings and workings of God within our hearts. Just like your closet contains your personal tastes and preferences for style, the way we live demonstrates the degree that we allow the divine work of God to permeate the different areas of our lives. In our study, we will look closely at the essentials necessary to produce a lifestyle that reflects the Father's heart.

The classic wardrobe is one that will stand the test of time. Fads come and go, enjoying their place in the sun for a season. Think about some of the fashions that we thought were must-haves at one time, but are now history. For instance, boat neck shirts, cowl neck and turtleneck sweaters, and the mock turtle neck. Pants also! You wouldn't be caught in "high waters" until they were called "crop style." Colors can be chic or not. In the 50s, red and pink together were taboo, but today they are considered stylish. There was a time when you never wore stripes with checks or plaids, but when the fashion gurus of the world send their models down the runway decked in a combo of these, they become all the rage. Fabrics also play a role in fashion. Denim was only worn by farmers until someone thought about pairing it with silk and rhinestones. But even while these fads are at the front, there is another style available that will always be right. This style is called "classic." For example, the color combination of black and white will work anytime and can be worn year after year without losing any glamor.

And so it is in a spiritual sense. Classic beauty is all about a timeless beauty that won't fade with age.

Chapter One

One
Miriam Models a Garment of Praise

God designed Miriam with a specific task in mind, just as He has crafted us for a unique purpose. Miriam's childhood was lived in times that were very troubled and dark. "Then Pharaoh gave this order to all his people: 'Every boy that is born you must throw into the Nile, but let every girl live'" (Exodus 1:22 NLT). Cruelty was the order of the day and everyone slaved for the king. Miriam lived in times when courage and faith in God were necessary to survive.

She was the "big sister" to baby Moses, who was miraculously allowed to live after he was discovered by the Pharaoh's daughter floating the Nile in a handcrafted vessel his parents had made. Moses was three months old and his crying had become hard to conceal, so his mom and dad made the little ark of bulrushes, placed Moses inside, and laid it in the reeds by the river's bank. Miriam took her post to watch what would happen when the Pharaoh's daughter came to bathe. Can you imagine the terror in this little girl as the baby boy she had cuddled was found by the daughter of the very one who had issued the command that all Hebrew baby boys be killed at birth? Our Heavenly Father was also watching and put a compassionate heart into the Egyptian princess. When Miriam asked if she could get a Hebrew nurse for the baby, God's favor was at work as she confirmed that would be fine. Back at home, Moses' mom was probably doing whatever she could to keep her mind occupied when Miriam burst on the scene, bubbling with excitement that she would be reunited with her little son as his nurse.

Miriam's childhood may have been lived in times of great turmoil, but according to the Bible, she also lived in times of great faith. "By faith Moses, when he was born, was hidden three months by his parents, because they saw *he was* a beautiful child; and they were not afraid of the king's command" (Hebrews 11:23 NKJV). Did Moses' parents know he was destined to be part of the deliverance God had promised to the Israelites? We don't know, but baby Moses being rescued out of the Nile was the result of an act of faith that influenced Miriam's life. Later, she was appointed to be a leader in Israel along with Moses and Aaron. Micah 6:4 (NKJV) says, "For I brought you up from the land of Egypt, I redeemed you from the house of bondage; And I sent before you Moses, Aaron, and Miriam."

Exodus 15:20-21 (NKJV) refers to Miriam as a prophetess. What is the role of Old Testament prophets and prophetesses? Their job is to proclaim God's Word, make prophetic revelations about the present or the future, and preach, encourage, comfort, and counsel. That is exactly what Miriam did. "Then Miriam the prophetess, the sister of Aaron, took the timbrel in her hand; and all the women went out after her with timbrels and with dances. And Miriam answered them: 'Sing to the LORD, For He has triumphed gloriously! The horse and its rider He has thrown into the sea!'"

I want to recognize Miriam's role as that of a praise and worship leader. Thus, her contribution to our classic wardrobe as women of God is a garment of praise.

Isaiah 61:1-3 (NIV) reads, "The Spirit of the Sovereign LORD is on me, because the LORD has anointed me to preach good news to the poor. He has sent me to bind up the broken-hearted, to proclaim freedom for the captives and release from darkness for the prisoners, to proclaim the year of the LORD's favor and the day of vengeance of our God, to comfort all who mourn, and provide for those who grieve in Zion—to bestow on them a crown of beauty instead of ashes, the oil of gladness instead of mourning, and a garment of praise instead of a spirit of despair. They will be called oaks of righteousness, a planting of the LORD for the display of his splendor."

Consider a garment of praise a natural addition to your closet. It would have to be your favorite bright and happy color that makes you feel good about yourself because praise does that for us. It is the opposite of despair.

One translation says that the garment of praise is for the spirit of heaviness. According to Psalms 100:4, a garment of praise could be considered royal attire for visiting the king: "Enter his gates with thanksgiving and his courts with praise; give thanks to him and praise his name." It's our choice to choose our clothes each day, just like it's our choice to choose praise each day. The benefits of such a choice are great.

Hebrews 13:15 (NKJV) says, "Therefore by Him let us continually offer the sacrifice of praise to God, that is, the fruit of *our* lips, giving thanks to His name." Praise and thanksgiving are to be in our conversation daily. As we offer praise to God, giving of thanks will accompany it. Here's some interesting information found in a secular publication that simply verifies what a great truth this act of praise is.

"Readers' Digest Oct. 2007
The most important words you'll say today…
The Science of Thank You can change your life!

Research proves that consciously grateful people…
- felt better about their lives
- were more optimistic
- were more energetic
- were more enthusiastic
- were more determined
- were more interested
- were more joyful
- exercised more
- had fewer illnesses
- got more sleep
- were more likely to have helped someone else.

Notice this Hebrew passage refers to continually offering the sacrifice of praise. Now, most of us don't want anything to do with sacrifice, but this sacrifice is really for our good. But it *is* a sacrifice, because when we need it the most is when it's hardest for us to praise. Praise stills the avenger and looses the power of God.

2 Chronicles 20:13-25 (NKJV) is a great testimonial of what praise can do. "Now all Judah, with their little ones, their wives, and their children, stood before the LORD." Many of us can identify with the pain of a family

crisis, and remember when we went before the Lord with our kids and husbands knowing the only solution to our situation was in the hands of our Heavenly Father. God's answer to Jehosophat was not to fear or be dismayed because in the words of the prophet, "The Lord is with you." Verses 21 and 22 say, "And when he had consulted with the people, he appointed those who should sing to the LORD, and who should praise the beauty of holiness, as they went out before the army and were saying: 'Praise the LORD, For His mercy *endures* forever.' Now when they began to sing and to praise, the LORD set ambushes against the people of Ammon, Moab, and Mount Seir, who had come against Judah; and they were defeated."

A New Testament example of the power of praise can be found in the book of Acts. Acts 16:25-26 (NKJV) states, "But at midnight Paul and Silas were praying and singing hymns to God, and the prisoners were listening to them. Suddenly there was a great earthquake, so that the foundations of the prison were shaken; and immediately all the doors were opened and everyone's chains were loosed."

Another thought on the power of praise is in Psalms 50:23 (NLT). "He who sacrifices thank-offerings honors me, and he prepares the way so that I may show him the salvation of God." Included in this salvation are deliverance, safety, welfare, prosperity, and victory.

Some items are a must for the wardrobe of a classy lady. I believe as women of God, our lives must be adorned with the garment of praise. We should never leave home without it!

Chapter Two

Two
Deborah, A Woman of Strength

"She girds herself with strength [spiritual, mental, and physical fitness for her God-given task] and makes her arms strong and firm" (Proverbs 31:17 AMP).

Our first lady, Miriam, is most remembered as a praise and worship leader. Praise is comely to the upright. That simply means that praise looks good! It's something that is flattering to all. Tall, short, big, little, thin, fat, or any size at all looks good when praise is the attire. In fact, a garment of praise will replace a spirit of heaviness and bring the oil of joy into our lives. And remember, one is not completely dressed without a smile upon his or her face! Never leave home without it.

Deborah's contribution to our classic wardrobe is strength. First of all, a definition of strength is needed. Obviously, those people working out vigorously at the gym have some strength. Their fitness marks them as people who are strong in a physical sense. But strength for the Proverbs lady is better defined as the power to resist strain and stress. It is toughness, durability, and the ability to resist psychological attacks. This woman has mental toughness and weathers the storms of life without crumbling under pressure.

Her assignment was to settle issues for the people as they lined up dailly to hear her advice. The Israelites would visit her under the Palm of Deborah and receive her counsel for their problems and circumstances.

On one particular day, Deborah gave a prophetic word to Barak. She told him that God would give him victory over Sisera, the enemy. But Barak would only commit to this plan of combat if Deborah would agree to go with him. She agreed but made it clear that if she went, Barak would receive no honor. Evidently, Barak had such great confidence in Deborah that he still insisted she accompany him even if it meant no recognition for him. The Word from God that Deborah had spoken to Barak happened exactly as it had been told and it was a great victory for Israel.

This Deborah was that lady that is admired by many. In the time of trouble, she never wavered. She was rock steady through it all. What enabled her to to be such a woman of magnificent courage? Not only was she willing to be God's messenger and be a listener to peoples' problems, but she was willing to even go to battle. Deborah had an inner quality that kept her cool under pressure with focused stability. Her reverent and worshipful fear of the Lord was the powerhouse of her life.

The book of Judges contains the account of the events of Deborah's life that portray her as a woman of strength. "Judges" were raised up by God to deliver a local tribe of Israel from apostasy and then govern them. God designed Deborah with a specific task in mind just as He designed you and me with a distinct purpose. One minister said they believed that as servants of God, we perform many things for Him in a lifetime, but only a single event would be the crown jewel of our achievements. Remember Mordecai's description of Esther: "Yet who knows whether you have come to the kingdom for such a time as this?" (Esther 4:14 NKJV). Much preparation took place before Esther exposed the plots of the enemy. We should be encouraged to know that our Heavenly Father has plans for us which may include the deliverance of a few people or even a nation.

Deborah was the only woman sanctioned by God to hold a position of leadership in Israel. No other "Judge" was ever called a prophet.

Chapter Three

Three
Ruth, Woman of Constancy

A WELL-DRESSED WOMAN SEEMS TO HAVE IT ALL TOGETHER. As we study the Proverbs lady, we can see how her wardrobe contained the essentials for a classic style. Clothes that stand the test of time and don't lose their beauty with the next fad.

Miriam's secret to being a woman of virtue and excellence was the garment of praise. Even the best-dressed chick isn't "all that" if she is sullen and sad. Praise dismisses the spirit of heaviness which comes to make life miserable for us. Women of God know the secret of great success comes from a life of praise: adorning situations with hope for the future instead of the gloom of the past. Praise lifts us out of the mundane circumstances we face and moves us ahead in life. Realizing the importance of eternal consequences is always a priority when faced with the challenge of the temporary. In fact, it is our responsibility as women of excellence.

Deborah learned how to attire herself with strength, which is a coordinate of the praise garment. Strength is an attribute that comes as we choose the life of praise. Daily, she did business under a palm tree, and her workday began before her clients came calling for advice. Being portrayed as a woman of godly wisdom means she must have spent precious time with the Master. The Secret Place had to be her first order of the day. A woman with military skill is a woman of extraordinary strength. Where did she find the secret of her strength? The Bible says it comes because of praise.

"Out of the mouth of babes and sucklings hast thou ordained **strength** because of thine enemies, that thou mightest still the enemy and the avenger" (Psalm 8:2 KJV).

Note that strength is interchangeable with praise in the margin of NIV and KJ versions.

Don't you love it when the things in your closet can be interchanged and look fantastic with all your other stuff? Jennifer, my daughter, is the master of buying fabrics and colors that work well with her favorite things.

"Many daughters have done virtuously, nobly and well (with the strength of character that is steadfast in goodness) but you excel them all. Charm and grace are deceptive, and beauty is vain because it is not lasting, but a woman who reverently and worshipfully fears the Lord, she shall be praised!" (Proverbs 31:29 AMP).

Ruth, challenged by circumstances, put her past behind her. She forsook her pagan heritage to cling to the people of Israel and the God of Israel.

Ruth 1:16-18 (NIV) says, "But Ruth replied, 'Don't urge me to leave you or to turn back from you. Where you go I will go, and where you stay I will stay. Your people will be my people and your God my God. Where you die I will die, and there I will be buried. May the LORD deal with me, be it ever so severely, if anything but death separates you and me.' When Naomi realized that Ruth was determined to go with her, she stopped urging her."

Moab culture—know who you are and be strong in it. When we follow God, He directs. Ruth 2:1-3 (NKJV) recounts, "There was a relative of Naomi's husband, a man of great wealth, of the family of Elimelech. His name *was* Boaz. So Ruth the Moabitess said to Naomi, 'Please let me go to the field, and glean heads of grain after *him* in whose sight I may find favor.' And she said to her, 'Go, my daughter.' Then she left, and went and gleaned in the field after the reapers. And she happened to come to the part of the field *belonging* to Boaz, who *was* of the family of Elimelech."

The door to tomorrow is opened by faith. The Israelites couldn't enter into His rest because of unbelief. Hebrews 3:12-19 (NKJV) remarks, "Beware, brethren, lest there be in any of you an evil heart of unbelief in departing from the living God; but exhort one another daily, while it is called "Today," lest any of you be hardened through the deceitfulness of sin. For we have become partakers of Christ if we hold the beginning of our confidence steadfast to the end, while it is said: 'Today, if you will hear His voice, Do not harden your hearts as in the rebellion.' For who, having heard, rebelled? Indeed, *was it* not all who came out of Egypt, *led* by Moses? Now with whom was He angry forty years? *Was it* not with those who sinned, whose corpses fell in the wilderness? And to whom did He swear that they would not enter His rest, but to those who did not obey? So we see that they could not enter in because of unbelief."

Ruth followed her mother-in-law's instructions concerning her tomorrow. Ruth never let the unknown of the future dismiss her dream. She committed to Naomi and her God and never looked back.

Ruth's secret to being a virtuous woman was that she was a woman of constancy. Offered the heritage of her past, she refused, and after vowing her loyalty to Naomi, she never changed. Constancy can be a key to our future as well. The lessons in Ruth are well worth taking to heart.

As for the end of the story, Ruth lived happily ever after. Ruth and Boaz had a son who they named Obed, and Ruth became the great-grandmother of David.

In the end, the rewards of Ruth's constancy were:
1. A new husband (Boaz)
2. A son (Obed)
3. A privileged position in the lineage of David and Christ (Obed was Jesse's dad and David the King was the son of Jesse...)

Chapter Four

Four
Hannah the Ideal Mother

Fashion First is a priority for women especially during different times of their lives. That first date, the first job, their wedding day, a family portrait or a family reunion, and countless other occasions that compel us to shop for the most becoming and most fashionable outfit. The goal of looking good on the outside will even send us to the gym for workouts, to the salon for manicures and pedicures, and to the diet center for a menu to make us the best size. Some of us braver ones will even have surgical procedures done to achieve the "look." We dedicate many hours, days, weeks, and months to have the same appearance that is in Vogue. And how we look *is* very important, but the Bible says that more important than the outward appearance is the condition of the heart. We can learn a few lessons here in many of the books of the Bible.

1 Peter 3:1-5 (NKJV) declares, "Wives, likewise, be submissive to your own husbands, that even if some do not obey the word, they, without a word, may be won by the conduct of their wives, when they observe your chaste conduct accompanied by fear. Do not let your adornment be merely outward—arranging the hair, wearing gold, or putting on fine apparel—rather let it be the hidden person of the heart, with the incorruptible beauty of a gentle and quiet spirit, which is very precious in the sight of God. For in this manner, in former times, the holy women who trusted in God also adorned themselves, being submissive to their own husbands...."

1 Corinthians 4:16-18 (NKJV) states, "Therefore we do not lose heart. Even though our outward man is perishing, yet the inward man is being renewed day by day. For our light affliction, which is but for a moment, is working for us a far more exceeding and eternal weight of glory, while we do not look at the things which are seen, but at the things which are not seen. For the things which are seen are temporary, but the things which are not seen are eternal."

Out of the mouth of two or three witnesses may every word be established. So, here are two references to the more valuable quality of life which is the spiritual. Our Proverbs lady excelled because she reverently and worshipfully feared the Lord.

Proverbs 31:29 (AMP) reads, "Many daughters have done virtuously, nobly and well (with the strength of character that is steadfast in goodness) but you excel them all. Charm and grace are deceptive, and beauty is vain because it is not lasting but a woman who reverently and worshipfully fears the Lord, she shall be praised!"

The ideal mother or the ideal woman in God's perspective would be the one whose priority in life is her relationship and fellowship with the Lord. Inviting the intervention of divine perspective will indeed change not only our lives on a personal level, but can even affect generations to come.

Hannah could be called the ideal mother because she had a heart for God. Her prayer for Samuel has even had an effect on our lives today because of his prophetic influence.

So it came to pass in the process of time that Hannah conceived and bore a son, and called his name Samuel, saying, 'Because I have asked for him from the LORD'" (1 Samuel 1:20 NKJV).

A look at Hannah's life shows us a sad situation. A hopeless situation. She was barren, and this marked her as one not favored by the Lord because her peers said the Lord closed her womb. Today, a woman could undergo fertility treatment and become pregnant, but for Hannah, being childless meant growing old and leaving nothing of her life behind for future generations. Her husband tried to console her and tell her that she had him in her life, who was better than many sons. Her rival, Elkannah's other wife, constantly goaded Hannah and kept a jealous spirit alive. Hannah's natural life was one of sorrow and hopelessness, so she prayed.

Eli watched her. He accused her of drunkenness. She explained, and then Eli granted her petition. 1 Samuel 1:10-17 (NKJV) tells us, "In bitterness of soul Hannah wept much and prayed to the LORD. And she made a vow, saying, 'O LORD Almighty, if you will only look upon your servant's misery and remember me, and not forget your servant but give her a son, then I will give him to the LORD for all the days of his life, and no razor will ever be used on his head.' As she kept on praying to the LORD, Eli observed her mouth. Hannah was praying in her heart, and her lips were moving but her voice was not heard. Eli thought she was drunk and said to her, 'How long will you keep on getting drunk? Get rid of your wine.' 'Not so, my lord,' Hannah replied, 'I am a woman who is deeply troubled. I have not been drinking wine or beer; I was pouring out my soul to the LORD. Do not take your servant for a wicked woman; I have been praying here out of my great anguish and grief.' Eli answered, 'Go in peace, and may the God of Israel grant you what you have asked of him.'"

A turnaround happened for Hannah after that. A total victory. Thanks be to God who always causes me to triumph!

Job 5 (Message Bible) says,
"God is famous for great and unexpected acts,
    There is no end to His surprises.
He gives rain, for instance, across the wide earth,
    and water to irrigate the fields.
He raises up the down and out,
    Gives firm footing to those sinking in grief.
He aborts the schemes of conniving crooks,
    so that none of their plots come to term.
He catches the know-it-alls in their conspiracies,
    all that intricate intrigue swept out with the trash!
Suddenly they are disoriented, plunged into darkness,
    they can't see to put one foot in front of the other.
But the downtrodden are saved by God,
    saved from the murderous plots, saved from the iron fist.
And so the poor continue to hope,
    while injustice is bound and gagged."

Naturally speaking, there was no answer for Hannah. However, when we are in impossible circumstances, we must know that we serve a God of possibility.

Smith Wigglesworth says that the only way to avoid the trap of the natural man is to be filled and continually filled with the spirit.

What is the trap of the natural man? Natural reasoning, sense, knowledge, and the inability to see beyond what is dictated by the voice of the carnal thoughts.

1 Corinthians 2:14 (NKJV) proclaims, "But the natural man does not receive the things of the Spirit of God, for they are foolishness to him; nor can he know them, because they are spiritually discerned."

Filled with the Spirit

Acts 2:1-4 (NKJV) recalls, "When the Day of Pentecost had fully come, they were all with one accord in one place. And suddenly there came a sound from heaven, as of a rushing mighty wind, and it filled the whole house where they were sitting. Then there appeared to them divided tongues, as of fire, and one sat upon each of them. And they were all filled with the Holy Spirit and began to speak with other tongues, as the Spirit gave them utterance."

Acts 10:44-47 (NKJV) says, "While Peter was still speaking these words, the Holy Spirit fell upon all those who heard the word. And those of the circumcision who believed were astonished, as many as came with Peter, because the gift of the Holy Spirit had been poured out on the Gentiles also. For they heard them speak with tongues and magnify God. Then Peter answered, 'Can anyone forbid water, that these should not be baptized who have received the Holy Spirit just as we have?'"

Acts 19:1-7 (NKJV) affirms, "And it happened, while Apollos was at Corinth, that Paul, having passed through the upper regions, came to Ephesus. And finding some disciples he said to them, 'Did you receive the Holy Spirit when you believed?' So they said to him, 'We have not so much as heard whether there is a Holy Spirit.' And he said to them, 'Into what then were you baptized?' So they said, 'Into John's baptism.' Then Paul said, 'John indeed baptized with a baptism of repentance, saying to the people that they should believe on Him who would come after him, that is, on Christ Jesus.' When they heard this, they were baptized in the name of the Lord Jesus. And when Paul had laid hands on them, the Holy Spirit came upon them, and they spoke with tongues and prophesied. Now the men were about twelve in all."

So far, here are the lessons we have learned:

1. Miriam is noted for her "garment of praise" as she led the Israelites in worship. The garment of praise is essential for a classic wardrobe because it can deliver us from impossible circumstances.
2. Deborah's contribution to our closet is strength. As a warrior and a fighter, she was confident in God, and that was the secret of her strength. When we put our trust in Him, we will never be disappointed or put to shame. Confidence is a must for women who trust God.
3. Ruth, a woman of constancy, couldn't be moved from her decision to follow Naomi and the God of Naomi. Her rewards still speak today. Know who you are (in Him) and be strong in it. Today's godly women are not wishy-washy; they are single-minded trusting in God.
4. Hannah poured out her heart to the Lord and became acquainted with He who supernaturally comes to our help and defense. A classic wardrobe designed by God will have the touch of the miracle-working power of our Heavenly Father. Today's woman of God will not be limited by a natural way of thinking.

Chapter Five

Five
The Shunammite, Mrs. Hospitality

2 Kings 4:8-17 (NKJV) imparts this story upon us: "One day Elisha went to Shunem. And a well-to-do woman was there, who urged him to stay for a meal. So whenever he came by, he stopped there to eat. She said to her husband, 'I know that this man who often comes our way is a holy man of God. Let's make a small room on the roof and put in it a bed and a table, a chair and a lamp for him. Then he can stay there whenever he comes to us.' One day when Elisha came, he went up to his room and lay down there. He said to his servant Gehazi, 'Call the Shunammite.' So he called her, and she stood before him. Elisha said to him, 'Tell her, "You have gone to all this trouble for us. Now what can be done for you? Can we speak on your behalf to the king or the commander of the army?"' She replied, 'I have a home among my own people.' 'What can be done for her?' Elisha asked. Gehazi said, 'Well, she has no son and her husband is old.' Then Elisha said, 'Call her.' So he called her, and she stood in the doorway. 'About this time next year,' Elisha said, 'you will hold a son in your arms.' 'No, my lord,' she objected. 'Don't mislead your servant, O man of God!' But the woman became pregnant, and the next year about that same time she gave birth to a son, just as Elisha had told her."

She was a well-to-do woman. Notable, great, and important—a great contrast to the first woman mentioned in this chapter. Still, Elisha asked, "What shall I do for you?"

Everyone is in need of something, those notable and important and also those whose circumstances are not so desirable. 2 Kings 4:1-7 (NKJV) gives the account of a woman whose circumstances were quite the contrast to the wealthy Shunnamite who built onto her house to accommodate the man of God, Elisha. This first woman mentioned here in 2 Kings 4:1 was mourning the death of her husband and dealing with creditors who were threatening to take her sons. She had no means to change her situation.

"The wife of a man from the company of the prophets cried out to Elisha, 'Your servant my husband is dead, and you know that he revered the LORD. But now his creditor is coming to take my two boys as his slaves.' Elisha replied to her, 'How can I help you? Tell me, what do you have in your house?' 'Your servant has nothing there at all,' she said, 'except a little oil.' Elisha said, "Go round and ask all your neighbors for empty jars. Don't ask for just a few. Then go inside and shut the door behind you and your sons. Pour oil into all the jars, and as each is filled, put it to one side.' She left him and afterward shut the door behind her and her sons. They brought the jars to her and she kept pouring. When all the jars were full, she said to her son, 'Bring me another one.' But he replied, 'There is not a jar left.' Then the oil stopped flowing. She went and told the man of God, and he said, 'Go, sell the oil and pay your debts. You and your sons can live on what is left.'"

Our God is beautiful for the situation. Such great contrast of these two ladies, but what did they have in common? Both were submissive to the Lord.

The Shunammite recognized the Man of God. She built a room for him. She said whenever He comes by, he can stay here. It will always be available. This is similar tothe New and Old Testament ministry of the Holy Spirit. Until Jesus came, people didn't have constant access to God or the kingdom of Heaven. The divine link of communication is shown through her story as well as His.

Her hospitality brought hospitality to her. Her kindness led to the asking, "What can be done for her?" A good word to the King? Or the commander of the Army? She had no son and her husband was old. Back then (and even now), sons were the builder of the family name as well as the heritage. Without a son, she had nothing to leave behind for future generations.

She received the prophet's reward. Jesus teaches about this in Matthew 10:40-42 (NKJV). "He who receives you receives Me, and he who receives Me receives Him who sent Me. He who receives a prophet in the name of a prophet shall receive a prophet's reward. And he who receives a righteous man in the name of a righteous man shall receive a righteous man's reward. And whoever gives one of these little ones only a cup of cold water in the name of a disciple, assuredly, I say to you, he shall by no means lose his reward."

The prophet's reward is supernatural. It's beyond man's ability. The Shunammite became pregnant and a son was born. But then, a tragedy... The child grew, and one day he went out to his father, who was with the reapers. 'My head! My head!' he said to his father. His father told a servant, 'Carry him to his mother.' After the servant had lifted him up and carried him to his mother, the boy sat on her lap until noon, and then he died" (II Kings 4:18-20 NLT).

Perhaps you can relate to this. The reward has come. Victory has manifested, and then just as you begin to get comfortable enjoying this gift from God, a devastating storm arrives and it looks like the glory is gone. It seems like defeat is certain and hope is nowhere on the horizon.

But this lady doesn't accept the death of her dream. Verse 21-28 tells us, "She went up and laid him on the bed of the man of God, then shut the door and went out. She called her husband and said, 'Please send me one of the servants and a donkey so I can go to the man of God quickly and return.' "Why go to him today?' he asked. 'It's not the New Moon or the Sabbath.' 'It's all right,' she said. She saddled the donkey and said to her servant, 'Lead on; don't slow down for me unless I tell you.' So she set out and came to the man of God at Mount Carmel. When he saw her in the distance, the man of God said to his servant Gehazi, 'Look! There's the Shunammite! Run to meet her and ask her, "Are you all right? Is your husband all right? Is your child all right?"' 'Everything is all right,' she said. When she reached the man of God at the mountain, she took hold of his feet. Gehazi came over to push her away, but the man of God said, 'Leave her alone! She is in bitter distress, but the LORD has hidden it from me and has not told me why.' 'Did I ask you for a son, my lord?" she said. 'Didn't I tell you, "Don't raise my hopes"?'"

The Shunammite trusted God as surely as the Lord lives. "But the child's mother said, 'As surely as the LORD lives and as you live, I will not leave you.' So he got up and followed her".

God speaks to us and puts dreams into our hearts that no man even knows. Dreams are so precious that we don't dare speak them. Mary pondered in her heart. As women, we understand how she nurtured the words of the angel because we do the same. The Shunammite said, "I will not leave you." Determined faith doesn't let the promise go. As a result, her dream was restored in 32-37 (NIV).

"When Elisha reached the house, there was the boy lying dead on his couch. He went in, shut the door on the two of them, and prayed to the LORD. Then he got on the bed and lay upon the boy, mouth to mouth, eyes to eyes, hands to hands. As he stretched himself out upon him, the boy's body grew warm. Elisha turned away and walked back and forth in the room and then got onto the bed and stretched out upon him once more. The boy sneezed seven times and opened his eyes. Elisha summoned Gehazi and said, 'Call the Shunammite.' And he did. When she came, he said, 'Take your son.' She came in, fell at his feet, and bowed to the ground. Then she took her son and went out."

The Shunammite made room for the Holy Spirit. How important is it in our lives that we also make room for His divine presence in our lives? As she did that, she became pregnant with the gift of God and her dreams came true. No one knew how she longed for a baby boy. No one knew how delighted she was at his birth. It was her secret desire, and only her Heavenly Father could provide it. And her dream came true! God's faithfulness can be trusted, and when the devil came to steal the miracle that had come, she was determined not to let it go.

Chapter Six

Six
Huldah, Trusted with God's Secret

1 Peter 3:3-5 (NKJV) says, "Do not let your adornment be merely outward—arranging the hair, wearing gold, or putting on fine apparel—rather let it be the hidden person of the heart, with the incorruptible beauty of a gentle and quiet spirit, which is very precious in the sight of God. For in this manner, in former times, the holy women who trusted in God also adorned themselves..."

The Proverbs 31 lady is recognized in the Amplified Bible. It reads, "Many daughters have done virtuously, nobly, and well (with the strength of character that is steadfast in goodness) but you excel them all. Charm and grace are deceptive, and beauty is vain because it is not lasting but a woman who reverently and worshipfully fears the Lord, she shall be praised!"

So far, here are the spiritual "must-haves" for your closet:

1. Garment of praise (Miriam).
2. Deborah's quality was her strength.
3. Ruth was a picture of commitment.
4. Hannah's life defined God as our supernatural helper.
5. The Shunnammite made room for God.

2 Kings 22:14 (NKJV) mentions Huldah, who was trusted with God's secret. Hilkiah the priest, Ahikam, Achbor, Shaphan, and Asaiah went to Huldah the prophetess. She was the wife of Shallum the son of Tikvah, who was the son of Harhas, and the keeper of the wardrobe (she dwelt in Jerusalem in the Second Quarter). They went to her and they spoke with her.

The setting was Jerusalem during the reign of Josiah who had become King at the age of eight. So, what prompted King Josiah to consult Huldah?

2 Kings 22:3 (NLT) explains, "In the eighteenth year of His reign, King Josiah sent the secretary, Shaphan, son of Azaliah, the son of Meshullam, to the temple of the Lord. He said, 'Go up to Hilkiah, the high priest, and have him get ready the money that has been brought into the temple of the Lord, which the doorkeepers have collected from the people. Have them entrust it to the men appointed to supervise the work on the temple. And have these men pay the workers who repair the temple of the Lord— the carpenters, the builders, and the masons. Also, have them purchase timber and dressed stone to repair the temple. But they need not account for the money entrusted to them, because they are acting faithfully.'

Hilkiah the high priest said to Shaphan the secretary, 'I have found the Book of the Law in the temple of the Lord.' He gave it to Shapthan, who read it. Then Shaphan the secretary went to the king and reported to him: 'Your officials have paid out the money that was in the temple of the Lord and have entrusted it to the workers and supervisors at the temple.' Then Shaphan informed the king, 'Hilkiah the priest has given me a book.' And Shaphan read from it in the presence of the king.

When the king heard the words of the Book of the Law, he tore his robes and sent servants to go and inquire of the Lord for me and for the people and for all Judah about what is written in this book that has been found. Great is the Lord's anger that burns against us because our fathers have not obeyed the words of this book."

Today, consultants are in demand for their inside information to revive businesses, organize affairs, put relationships in order, and so on. Consultants are experts in certain areas and will come to your aid for a hefty price. Evidently, Huldah was known for such an ability, but her insight was a gift from God rather than the result of secular study and knowledge.

1 Corinthians 12:1-11 (NLT) states, "Now about spiritual gifts, brothers, I do not want you to be ignorant. You know that when you were pagans, somehow or other you were influenced and led astray to mute idols. Therefore I tell you that no-one who is speaking by the Spirit of God says, 'Jesus be cursed,' and no-one can say, 'Jesus is Lord,' except by the Holy Spirit. There are different kinds of gifts, but the same Spirit. There are different kinds of service, but the same Lord. There are different kinds of working, but the same God works all of them in all men. Now to each one the manifestation of the Spirit is given for the common good. To one there is given through the Spirit the message of wisdom, to another the message of knowledge by means of the same Spirit, to another faith by the same Spirit, to another gifts of healing by that one Spirit, to another miraculous powers, to another prophecy, to another distinguishing between spirits, to another speaking in different kinds of tongues, and to still another the interpretation of tongues. All these are the work of one and the same Spirit, and he gives them to each one, just as he determines."

Huldah was not a prominent woman except for the significant message she gave to the king. Hence, she is not mentioned in Hebrews' Hall of Faith. We are not all going to be in the limelight like Joyce Meyers or Gloria Copeland, but we are all a part of God's design and He has certain purposes for each of us to fill. God's secrets are found as we visit Him in the Secret Place. Wonderful things will be revealed to us because of our living contact.

God's classic beauty is trustworthy. Ephesians 4:22 (NKJV) says, "...put on the new self-created to be like God in true righteousness and holiness." The clothes in our closets didn't just happen to appear; we purposely chose them. In the same fashion (no pun intended), the qualities we are known for are the result of the choices we make.

Remember:

1. The garment of praise is my choice!
2. Strength is in me because I choose to keep close communion with God.
3. Commitment to follow God and keep His Word is a choice.
4. Supernatural help is mine as I pour out my heart to the Lord and recognize Him as my Helper.
5. Making room for God by prayer, worship, and study is my choice.
6. Being trustworthy enough to receive God's gifts and secrets is evident when we position ourselves in the Secret Place.

Chapter Seven

Seven
Esther, Risk Taker

WHAT WOULD CAUSE A PERSON TO RISK THEIR OWN LIFE FOR OTHERS? ESTHER'S willingness will be revealed as we look behind the scenes and see God's interests, purposes, and confident care of His people. Esther was a young Jewish girl who became Queen of the Persian Empire. Because of her position, she was in a place to prevent the annihilation of her entire nation. Possibly the most memorable words spoken in this book are Mordecai's when he said to her, "Who knows whether you have come to the kingdom for such a time as this?"

Understand that born-again women today are just as much a part of God's plan as Esther was, and no one else in the kingdom can do what you've been chosen to do. So, who knows whether you have come to the kingdom for such a time as this? We should regard these words as we daily walk out our time here on Earth.

Esther's beginning was not one of great promise. She was orphaned and then adopted by her cousin, Mordecai. Described as a certain Jew in Shushan, Mordecai stepped into Esther's life when her parents died. Certain circumstances brought Esther into a place of royalty. She was the classic "rags to riches" story.

It all started when Vashti defied the king. 180 days of celebration were closing with a feast for all people—great and small—in the capital, Shushan, in the garden of the king's palace. Imagine the environmental decor: hangings of fine white cloth, of green and blue cotton fastened with cords of fine linen and purple to silver rings or rods and marble pillars. Couches or beds of gold and silver, upon a pavement of red and blue and white, and black marble. The drinks were served in vessels of gold, and no two were alike. The king wanted to show off the queen, who was very beautiful.

Vashti lost her role as queen to King Ahasuerus when she wouldn't submit to his command to appear at his feast. Her disrespect to the king's wishes cost her everything. Esther's respect and submission to authority gave her everything.

How Esther became queen is a perfect Cinderella story. The decree was given that all the young beautiful virgins in all the provinces needed to be taken to the king's house under custody of Hegai, the king's eunuch. Esther had favor in Hegai's sight and was given seven maids and the best apartment in the harem.

Now is the perfect time for a quick session of Character Lesson 101: Always obey your parents. Esther didn't reveal her family identity or nationality because Mordecai told her not to, as said in Esther 2:10 (AMPC). "Esther had not made known her nationality or her kindred, for Mordecai had charged her not to do so." It is also repeated in Esther 2:20 (AMPC): "Now Esther had not yet revealed her nationality or her people, for she obeyed Mordecai's command to her to fear God and execute His commands just as when she was being brought up by him."

A night with the king was given to each girl who could also choose anything from the harem to take or wear into the king's presence. Whatever she chose, she could keep. Again, Esther's values are apparent in Esther 2:15 (AMPC) when she only required what Hegai suggested that she take. "Now when the turn for Esther the daughter of Abihail, the uncle of Mordecai who had taken her as his own daughter, had come to go in to the king, she required nothing but what Hegai the king's attendant, the keeper of the women, suggested. And Esther won favor in the sight of all who saw her."

When we wear the right apparel or when we bind truth, mercy, and love about our neck and write it on the table of our heart, we will find good understanding, high esteem, and favor in the sight of God and man.

Meanwhile, Mordecai sits at the king's gate and overhears two of the king's eunuchs plotting to kill the king. Mordecai told Esther, and she, in turn, told the king (in Mordecai's name). An investigation revealed it was true and the two eunuchs were hanged. The whole event was recorded in the book of Chronicles before the king.

This led to the development of Haman's plot. Haman got promotions above all the king's servants who bowed and revered him—except Mordecai. Letters were sent to destroy and kill all Jews (both young and old, little children and women) in one day and take spoil. When the writing was published, Mordecai put on sackcloth and ashes and cried with a loud and bitter cry.

Hatach (one of the king's chamberlains) was sent by Esther to Mordecai, who gave him a copy of the writing to take back to Esther with these words: "Go to the king and make supplication and request before him for her people." Esther 4:14 (AMPC) continues, "For if you remain silent at this time, relief and deliverance for the Jews will arise from another place, but you and your father's family will perish. And who knows but that you have come to a royal position for such a time as this?"

After a three-day fast, Esther made her appearance in royal apparel.

A banquet invitation was given only to the King and Haman. However, Haman couldn't enjoy it because of his discontentment towards Mordecai.

The gallows were built and prepared. A sleepless night was ahead as the Chronicles were read to the King. Haman returns to inform the King about the gallows for Mordecai but is met with unexpected news.

"What shall be done for the man the King delights to honor?" Haman answers with expectations that it is he the king is talking about.

- royal apparel
- a horse
- a crown
- a parade

"Honor shall be given to Mordecai." says the King

Hamaan is mortified.

Then, the king's chamberlains came to bring Haman to the banquet Esther had prepared. Esther 7:1-5 (AMPC) narrates, "So the king and Haman went to dine with Queen Esther, and as they were drinking wine on that second day, the king again asked, 'Queen Esther, what is your petition? It will be given you. What is your request? Even up to half the kingdom, it will be granted.' Then Queen Esther answered, 'If I have found favor with you, O king, and if it pleases your majesty, grant me my life—

this is my petition. And spare my people—this is my request. For I and my people have been sold for destruction and slaughter and annihilation. If we had merely been sold as male and female slaves, I would have kept quiet, because no such distress would justify disturbing the king.' King Xerxes asked Queen Esther, 'Who is he? Where is the man who has dared to do such a thing?'" Esther told the king that Haman was the adversary and the wicked enemy, so they hanged Haman on the gallows that he had prepared for Mordecai. All's well that ends well.

What will we wear to an appointment with the king? 1 Peter 3:3-5 (NKJV) tells us, "Do not let your adornment be merely outward—arranging the hair, wearing gold, or putting on fine apparel—rather let it be the hidden person of the heart, with the incorruptible beauty of a gentle and quiet spirit, which is very precious in the sight of God. For in this manner, in former times, the holy women who trusted in God also adorned themselves..."

Come into the holy of holies, enter by the blood of the Lamb. Don the Robes of righteousness and be present.

So, what made Esther willing to risk her life?

1. She was concerned with important things, not merely urgent things. She could have had the most valuable item in the harem, but she chose the king's desire rather than her own. Hegai knew the king's desire and Esther respected his advice.
2. She had a value system in her heart that molded her to be submissive to authority. Whenever Mordecai told her not to disclose her nationality or family heritage, she didn't question the reason. Rather, she hid the secret in her heart which later proved to be a trump card in the face of adversity.
3. Commitment was also woven into the fabric of Esther's heart. Being dedicated to doing the right thing is an important part of commitment, and was very obvious in her since she willingly went before the king without being called.

About the Author

Susan Bolding, along with her husband of fifty-six years, has nearly four decades of pastoral experience through Liberty Church El Dorado in Arkansas. As a certified public school teacher she has used her giftings to develop the children's ministry in their local church. Susan can also be seen on VTN, teaching how to practically apply the word of God to everyday living on, *The Bottom Line with Jim and Susan Bolding*.

Susan's study has led her to write, *Fashion* by Design because she saw the skillful ease and confidence displayed by the lady in Proverbs 31. Proverbs 31:29 (AMPC) says, "Many daughters have done virtuously, nobly, *and* well [with the strength of character that is steadfast in goodness], but you excel them all." As Christian women of God, we desire to live a lifestyle that reflects the Father's heart. We strive to be just like His daughters in the Bible. This book, first written as a Bible study, will enlighten you on how to live like a daughter of the King.

Someone once said that if we cultivate the presence of God in our personal lives, His power will be apparent in our public lives. We will embrace our Heavenly heritage when we set aside daily personal time with Him. Discover truths within *Fashion by Design* that will empower you to live every day in His presence. As you walk through the daily lives of these powerful women chosen by God, I pray you will see they chose to live for Him and become adorned with a *Classic Wardrobe* within.

Conclusion

As members of the Royal Family of God, we are daughters of the Most High, and we have inherited a legacy that cannot be bought with money. It's time for us to evaluate our wardrobes and consider how we present ourselves. Clearly, our Heavenly Father has provided us with luxurious garments at a price that no one could ever afford. I encourage you, as I will challenge myself, to dress each day in the designer attire we have received, fully paid for by the precious blood of the Lamb.

Prayer

Heavenly Father, I am so grateful to be called your child. Because I am yours, I represent you in my life on Earth. Help me recognize that everything will improve as I walk through each day, aware of the importance of adorning my heart. Let me be quick to hear your voice.

I choose to put on the garment of praise like Miriam, and I am thankful for the inner strength that you provide me, just as you strengthened Deborah. Lead me every day by your Holy Spirit, and help me remember to make room for you each day.

Like Ruth, let me be a woman of commitment and confidence. As I spend time in the Secret Place with you, may my life be defined by the supernatural help and guidance you gave to Huldah. I want to be an overcomer like Hannah, even when it seems there is no hope.

Lastly, let me be like Esther and be willing to take risks. Thank you, God; as I spend time with you in my private life, I trust that I will receive great rewards from you in my public life.

brush
PUBLISHING
& associates

www.ingramcontent.com/pod-product-compliance
Lightning Source LLC
Chambersburg PA
CBHW050045080526
44586CB00014B/1469